A CENTURY of
CHELTENHAM

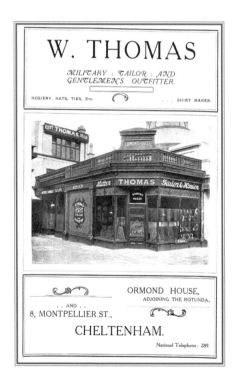

W. THOMAS

MILITARY : TAILOR : AND
GENTLEMEN'S OUTFITTER.

HOSIERY, HATS, TIES, Etc.   . . . SHIRT MAKER.

ORMOND HOUSE,
ADJOINING THE ROTUNDA,

. . AND . .
8, MONTPELLIER ST.,
CHELTENHAM.

National Telephone : 289.

Carriages wait in this 1908 picture of the Opera House (now the Everyman), which opened in Regent Street on 1 October 1891 with a performance by Lillie Langtry. Small of stature, though huge of reputation, the celebrated actress took centre stage and delivered a specially commissioned (and very long) poem in rhyming couplets. The theatre was designed by architect Frank Matcham – who was also responsible for the London Palladium – and was built in just six months. Ellen Terry, George Robey, John Gielgud, Margot Fonteyn and numerous other luminaries have performed on its stage – and the first talkie film seen in Cheltenham was screened at the theatre. (*Author's collection*)

A CENTURY of CHELTENHAM

ROBIN BROOKS

First published in the United Kingdom in 2001 by
Sutton Publishing Limited exclusively

This new paperback edition first published in 2012

The History Press
The Mill, Brimscombe Port
Stroud, Gloucestershire, GL5 2QG
www.thehistorypress.co.uk

British Library Cataloguing in Publication Data
A catalogue record for this book is available from the British Library.

ISBN 978-0-7524-7474-8

Illustrations

Front endpaper: Christchurch with St James's station in the background, *c.* 1930. *(Peter Stephens)*
Back endpaper: Sandford Lido, 1985. *(Brian Donnan Photography)*
Half title page: Military outfitters such as W. Thomas in Montpellier were kept busy supplying uniforms for young
officers when war against Germany was declared on 4 August 1914. The shop – it's a newsagent and grocer's today –
stood next door to the Rotunda, which was pressed into service as a club and canteen for volunteers. *(Mrs J. Chilton)*
Title page: For over a century the larger than life-size manikin of a Gordon Highlander – complete with kilt,
bearskin and sporran – stood guard outside
Wright's High Street shop. Cheltenham's famous
kilt wearer disappeared to London when Fred[k]
Wright's closed in 1987. Then he came up for
auction in 1990, was bought by the grandson
of the chap who founded Fred[k] Wright's, and
now you can visit him in the town's museum.
(Author's collection)

The Co-op's Bath Road branch, *c.* 1910. *(Gloucestershire Echo)*

Contents

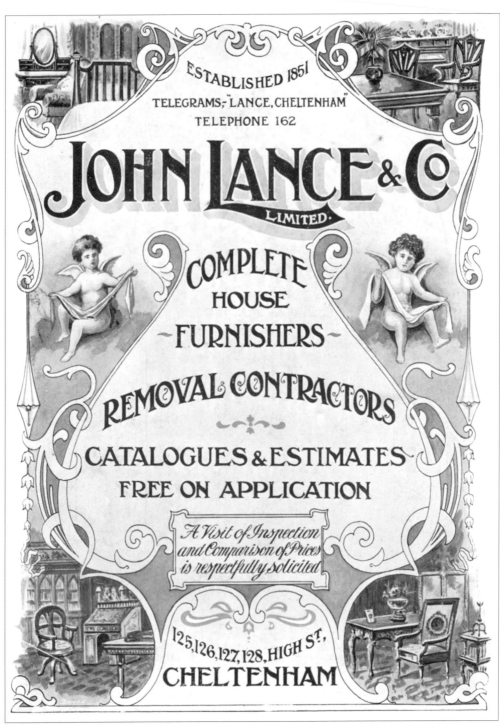

Advertisement for John Lance & Co. Ltd, 1908.

Introduction

'Prim, proper and poor' describe Cheltenham as it crossed the threshold of the twentieth century. The population, which stood at a little under 50,000, had grown rapidly in previous decades. But accounting for much of the increase were ex-colonial types – ageing and impecunious – home from the Raj to eke out their dotage. Cheltenham was known as 'The Anglo-Indian's paradise'. The town was in retirement and over the next twenty years the population fell.

The local economy was hardly vibrant either. House prices had slumped and in 1901 there were as many as 800 of the town's large houses empty or to let. Apart from domestic service, employment opportunities were few. Accommodation was also in short supply for

April 1900 was the first time Cheltenham saw motor vehicles in large numbers, when contestants in the Automobile Club of Great Britain and Ireland's 1,000-mile trial passed through the town. Cheltenham was chosen as a convenient stop-off stage midway between Bristol and Birmingham and drivers of the eighty-three vehicles – which represented 10 per cent of all the cars in the country – had lunch at the Queen's Hotel, where this photograph was taken. Forty-eight starters completed the course and the fastest time en route – a dashing 37.63 mph – was recorded by Sir Charles Rolls (of Rolls-Royce fame). *(Author's collection)*

The High Street, seen here in about 1910, has been at the centre of the town's commercial life for nigh on a thousand years. Until a couple of centuries ago, the High Street was pretty much all there was of Cheltenham, apart from a few alleyways that ran off this main artery. Three items of street furniture to notice in this picture are the town clock in the distance, the heart and honeysuckle design ironwork above the shop canopy in the foreground, and the onion and dragon lamp standards in between. *(Author's collection)*

working-class people and conditions in slums at the 'Lower Dockem' (west) end of town were grim.

When war against Germany was declared on 4 August 1914, Cheltenham was gripped by jingoistic euphoria. By October 1,400 locals had signed up, but the belief that 'it will be all over by Christmas' waned as the names of those killed took up ever more space in the local press.

It has often been written that the First World War put an end to the old order in Britain. So it did, but Cheltenham kept change at arm's length for a while longer. There's a story that in the 1920s – when the Promenade was considered strictly a no-go area for the hoi polloi – the prosperous owner of a stationery shop named Banks raised his hat to a minor-titled (and probably impecunious) lady customer on his way to work. In the following morning's post he received a letter of sharp rebuke from Madam, who made it quite clear that she did not wish to be acknowledged in public by a mere tradesman.

Francis Close declared 'That an institution for the training of masters and mistresses upon scriptural and evangelical principles in connection with the Church of England is urgently called for and that effort should be made to establish such a training college in Cheltenham'. In 1847, seven trainee teachers formed the nucleus of the new college. Female students first received training at the building in Lower High Street that had once been Cheltenham's hospital. In 1869, they moved to the newly built St Mary's Hall on the corner of St George's Place and Clarence Street, which was designed by J.T. Darby, architect of Cheltenham's Winter Gardens. Our picture shows Edwardian students in St Mary's Hall, later re-named Shaftesbury Hall. *(Peter Stephens)*

By 1930 Cheltenham was in the grip of a depression that shrouded much of the country. 'Overshadowing everything is the dark cloud of unemployment', reported the *Gloucestershire Chronicle*. Around 20 per cent of people were out of work and one of the few places where business was brisk was the Salvation Army soup kitchen in New Street, where 400 penny meals were served every day.

Some jobs were created by the clearance of slums in the west end of town and the development of new housing in Whaddon, St Marks, Pates Avenue and the Moors estate.

To great public approval, miles of track were removed from Cheltenham's roads, and trams trundled the town no more. They were replaced by motor buses, which local travellers boarded at the newly opened Royal Well bus station.

In January 1937, a traffic census recorded all vehicles passing along Cheltenham's High Street between 6 a.m. and 10 p.m. There were 6,869 cars, 7,408 bicycles and 174 horses.

By the end of the decade war was once more inevitable. In early September 1939, 2,000 evacuees, children and young mothers, arrived in Cheltenham from the Midlands. In the Promenade two 20,000-gallon water tanks appeared, to be used if the town centre were set ablaze by incendiary bombs.

'Eat George's bread', urges the advert that fronts the upper deck of a tram near Boots Corner, bound for Leckhampton. Trams first trundled Cheltenham's streets on 22 August 1901, an occasion that prompted an enthusiastic response from the *Gloucestershire Graphic*. 'At last the trams are here! Round the corner comes a huge noise like a small Town Hall on wheels and the quiet respectability of Cheltenham is challenged by the sharp ting-tang on the gong and grinding of the wheels on the rail grooves together with the cars' singing on the wires.' The jubilation was short lived. By the end of the 1920s trams had been rendered redundant by the quicker, go-anywhere bus. Most tram services ceased in March 1930 and the town's terminal tram ran just after dawn on Wednesday 31 December of that year. *(Peter Stephens)*

Cheltenham was the divisional control centre for Tewkesbury, Moreton-in-Marsh, Northleach and the area in between. This meant that services such as civil defence, air raid precautions (ARP), ambulance, fire fighting, the provision of ration books and special police were organised from the town. The nerve centre of the ARP was Shirers & Lances basement, and on the roof of the same department store an air-raid siren was positioned. Cheltenham was also HQ to the American Forces of Supply in the build-up to D-day and the town swarmed with Jeeps and GIs.

DEMOLITION DECADES

Cheltenham in the '50s was changing fast. The population stood at about 60,000 and was rising apace because of the good employment prospects presented by Dowty's, the recent arrival of GCHQ and engineering firms such as Walker Crossweller. To house the incomers, Hesters Way and Benhall gobbled up what had previously been open fields and humpty-dumps. In the town centre, large areas were being redeveloped.

This process continued throughout the 1960s, when the biggest swinger in town was the demolition man's hammer. Buildings that would be listed treasures today were reduced to rubble.

Among the razed were the boys' grammar school in the High Street along with its near neighbours, the Fleece Hotel and a row of characterful small shops. Down came the Gas Company's office on the corner of North Street and Albion Street. The imposing nineteenth-century offices of Shirers & Lances in Well Walk bit the dust. And Cheltenham's best example of Victorian Gothic domestic architecture, Tudor Lodge, was replaced in The Park by a row of square, flat-roofed town houses. Leckhampton and Charlton Kings lost their railway stations courtesy of Dr Beeching, along with St James and Malvern Road.

There's no doubt that Cheltenham is the poorer for losing so many fine buildings in the 1950s and '60s. And it's equally certain the town is still suffering from what the planners allowed to be built in those architecturally barren decades.

Cheltenham Borough Council was formed when, as a result of the reorganisation of local government in England and Wales in April 1974, Charlton Kings Urban District Council merged with Cheltenham Municipal Borough.

Soon after Montpellier Spa opened in 1809, the gardens opposite were laid out as a place of recreation for subscribers who took the waters. A bandstand and open air theatre were added, plus tennis courts when the gardens were acquired by the Borough Council in 1892. *(Peter Stephens)*

15

A sad loss to the town was H.H. Martyn & Company, which played a major role in the development of industry in Cheltenham and elsewhere in Gloucestershire. Founded in Cheltenham in 1888, the firm established a worldwide reputation for the quality of its art-craftsmanship in wood, metal, stone, glass and plaster. It built aeroplanes, cars, fitted out many of the world's great ocean liners, built the Speaker's chair in the House of Commons, the Cenotaph in Whitehall – and much more. Dowty's – and the Gloster Aircraft Company – were both offshoots of Martyn's.

The company probably represented the greatest concentration of craftsmanship and trade skills in the country – perhaps the world. But the demise of Britain's shipbuilding industry resulted in its parent company – Maple's – selling off Martyn's assets and closing the firm in 1971. The Sunningend works then became Lansdown Industrial Park.

The largest single development in Cheltenham during the 1980s was the Regent Arcade. It was built between 1982 and 1984 on the site of the forty-five-bedroomed Plough Hotel, an ancient coaching inn that fronted on the High Street, plus the yard and car park behind it.

The Promenade lost a landmark in the middle of the decade when the ABC cinema was pulled down to be replaced by Royscot House. But the new building was in sympathy with its neighbours and hinted that town planners had learned from the mistakes made in the previous three decades.

In 1990 Cheltenham made the record books when the summertime thermometer nudged 37.1° C, the highest temperature ever recorded in Britain.

Its population now tops 115,000, Cheltenham moved a step further towards a traffic-free centre when a further section of the High Street between Winchcombe Street and Pittville Street was paved over, along with part of Regent Street.

The Spa Shuttle arrived in – and departed from – Cheltenham in the late 1990s. Three 'Noddy trains', as the shuttles soon came to be called, provided a free ferry service to travellers around the town centre/Montpellier/Pittville areas. Some saw the gas-powered road trains as a far-sighted attempt to address the problem of traffic congestion. Others baulked at the cost and felt the Noddy trains made the problem worse by reducing the speed of vehicles in their wake to a snail's pace. The Shuttles were withdrawn in September 1999.

The twentieth century brought change at a faster rate than any before it. Cheltenham doubled its population, increased in area and diversified in function to become a commercial centre, the home of international festivals, a fashionable address – and as much a town of contrasts as it ever was.

But prim, proper and poor? No, not any more.

Edwardian Elegance

Years before the first Hollywood epic and decades before Pavarotti packed
Hyde Park, Cheltenham staged an extravaganza of saga-like proportions.
'The Gloucestershire Historical Pageant' of July 1908 took six days to
perform, featured a costumed cast of hundreds and engaged ranks of
massed musicians. This was a show of Edwardian grandeur at its imperial
mightiest. A full-scale castle constructed in Pittville Park provided the
backdrop, and against this performers presented no less than the entire
history of Britain in word, mime and song. This postcard reveals Queen
Elizabeth I wagging her finger at Sir Walter Raleigh. *(Author's collection)*

Horse-drawn carriages with liveried drivers at the reins pass this way and that along the Colonnade in the early years of the nineteenth century. Originally a row of half a dozen shops that left the High Street, the Colonnade was eventually extended to become the Promenade. To the right the art nouveau windows of Cavendish House – Cheltenham's first department store – are reflected in the pavement wet from a recent summer shower. When it opened in 1826 the shop was named Clark & Debenham's after the founding partners. *(Peter Stephens)*

The Promenade, *c.* 1910. In the same year that Cavendish House opened, the building you can see in this picture with railings round its front garden was built. It was home to a painter named Millet. When he packed his pallette and brushes the house became the Imperial Hotel, then in 1856 the Imperial Club for 'resident noblemen and gentlemen'. Many people will remember this address as that of Cheltenham's main post office, which it was from 1874 until 1987. In that year the GPO moved to the High Street and Hooper's acquired the Promenade premises. *(Peter Stephens)*

Delivery boys stand with their handcart in a dusty Prom during Edwardian days. Once eulogised by *The Times* as 'The most beautiful thoroughfare in Britain', the Promenade extends in a tree-lined, straight stretch for just over a quarter of a mile, bordered by broad pavements – fine shops to one side, buildings and grand gardens to the other. At the time of this photograph, the Prom was a no-go area for artisans and tradespeople during shopping hours. *(Gloucestershire Echo)*

The Promenade, seen here at a time when horse power had four legs. Early in the nineteenth century the land now occupied by the Prom was a marshy bog, boasting nothing more impressive than a few ramshackle cottages. In one of them the widow of British Prime Minister Spenser Percival came to live after her husband had the dubious distinction of being assassinated. He was shot on 11 May 1812 by a Liverpool banker named John Bellingham who was hanged for the crime eleven days later. *(Gloucestershire Echo)*

'Hello, hello. What's he doing with that camera?' The Prom – originally known as the Sherborne, or Imperial Promenade – began its existence as a walkway from Cheltenham's High Street to a spa pump room that stood where the Queen's Hotel now stands. It was laid out properly in 1818 and lined with forty-four chestnut trees. Then land along its length was sold for commercial and residential development. *(Gloucestershire Echo)*

The terrace on the left overlooking the Promenade Long Garden was built in 1825 as private houses and named Harward's Buildings. From 1914 onwards these houses were acquired and became the Municipal Offices. In the foreground can be seen the ornate frontage of the Imperial Rooms, originally a spa. It was moved to this position in 1837 and demolished to make way for the Regal cinema, which opened in 1939. *(Author's collection)*

Opposite: The Winter Garden was Cheltenham's own Crystal Palace and stood in Imperial Gardens. It was constructed in 1879 to a design by J.T. Darby with the intended purpose of providing 'A large concert room and other accessories, calculated to afford recreation and amusement to the upper classes'. In no time it became as clear as the glass roof that the upper classes had no wish to recreate or be amused there. The building was capable of accommodating huge hordes of people, but was largely unsuitable for anything much. It had the acoustic virtues of an aircraft hangar – and if it rained during a concert the thrumming on the glass roof did battle with the performers. The wonderful white elephant of a building was finally demolished in September 1940 by order of the town council. *(Author's collection)*

21

When the camera clicked on this High Street scene, the imposing stone building on the left had only recently opened as Lloyd's Bank. It was built in 1900 on the site of the Assembly Rooms, a venue for balls and entertainment that flourished in Cheltenham's high days as a fashionable spa.

A detail in the right foreground is a Penfold letter box, which became Post Office standard issue in 1866. About ninety of these remain in the country and Cheltenham has eight. *(Author's collection)*

Another Penfold letter box appears in this 1909 postcard of Cheltenham's Town Hall. The building was designed by the Gloucester architect Frederick Waller and built in 1903 to replace the Assembly Rooms. In an unsuccessful attempt to reverse the decline in popularity of Cheltenham as a health resort, the Central Spa was opened in the Town Hall in 1906. You can take the waters there to this day, but you'll have to help yourself. No longer are there maids in mob caps and frilly pinnies to serve the salty solution as there were in times gone by. *(Peter Stephens)*

In 1862 Charles Cook Higgs gave land for a new church and £1,000 towards the cost of building it. He expressed the wish that the remaining finance should be secured by public subscription, but the good people of Charlton Kings failed to delve deep into their pockets. So then application was made for funds to the Ecclesiastical Commissioners, who didn't rush for their cheque book either. In the end Charles Higgs paid the £7,000 building cost of Holy Apostles himself. John Middleton was the architect, whose work in the town includes St Mark's Church, Delancy hospital, the Ladies' College building in St George's Road and St Philip and St James's church. *(Peter Stephens)*

Neptune's Fountain, seen here in 1904, was designed by the borough engineer Joseph Hall. Modelled on Rome's Fontana di Trevi and carved from Portland stone by the local firm of R.L. Boulton, it first gushed on 30 October 1893. It commemorates nothing and is in memory of nobody, but was part of a general scheme to perk up the Prom. A town guide tells us 'It was installed when Victorian Gothicism was on the wane, with beaux arts influences gaining ground on a lingering neo-mediaevalism.' So there. *(Peter Stephens)*

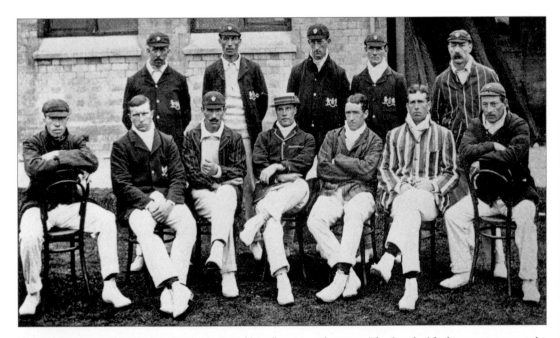

The Gloucesterhire cricket team in 1900 was captained by Gilbert Jessop, known as 'The Croucher' for his urgent stance at the wicket. That's him, front row centre in the straw hat. A resident of Cambray Place and a pupil of the boys' grammar school, Jessop is reputed to be one of the hardest hitters of the ball in cricketing history. At Bristol in 1901, playing for the county against the West Indies, he scored 157 in an hour. At the Cheltenham Festival of 1907 he scored 53 in 15 minutes and his 150 highest innings were made at the rate of 82 runs per hour. Jessop played for Burford a few times. On the last occasion he struck five balls so far outside the ground that none could be found. It was then that Burford had to ask Jessop not to play for them any more as the cost of replacing the balls lost by his powerful strokes threatened to bankrupt the club. (*Gloucestershire Echo*)

This portrait of the Cheltenham jockey Fred Archer and his wife appeared in the *Gloucestershire Chronicle & Graphic* in 1908, the year in which his mother died. Archer rose meteorically from humble origins to widespread celebrity. This son of a publican was on first-name terms with aristocrats and royalty. He earned vast sums and gambled big time. Scandal nipped at his heels, with mystery and intrigue often taking a chomp or two too. Then came personal tragedy on a scale usually only encountered in works of fiction – and death by his own hand at the age of twenty-nine. Perhaps the best memorial to this remarkable Cheltonian rests in the statistics of his career: 8,004 mounts, 2,148 wins. (*Gloucestershire Echo*)

Leckhampton railway station, seen here in 1902, opened with the completion of the Banbury line in 1881. In 1906, the Hatherley Loop was added, enabling trains from the north to pass through Leckhampton on to South Wales. A train named the Coast to Coast Express started on the LNER line from Newcastle, joined the GWR track from Cheltenham and continued to Cardiff. In the 1920s, Leckhampton station was given the grander title of Cheltenham South. Closure came in 1962 and today the site is an industrial park. *(Joe Stevens)*

Charlton Kings station, pictured in 1909, was designated a mere halt on OS sheet 144 maps. This was a touch derisory really, as the facilities included two platforms with a waiting room on each, a ticket office, gas lamps and permanent staff. Until quarrying ended in the late 1920s, a line ran the 1.25 miles from Charlton Kings to Leckhampton Hill. An 0–4–0 tank engine named Lightmoor, built by the Bristol firm of Peckett's, chuffed along the branch line with locally hewn limestone bound for building sites in distant places. Thanks to Dr Beeching the station closed in 1962 and today the site is an industrial park. *(Joe Stevens)*

The twin crowns of Highbury Congregational Church can be glimpsed above the rooftops in this pre-First World War view of Winchcombe Street. Behind the impressively bearded man in the cart, we can see that J. Webb's shop is number seven, while the Umbrella Manufactory next door is number seven-and-a-half. No doubt the young chap crossing the street had to pick his way carefully. Horse-drawn transport had its own kind of impact on the urban environment. *(Author's collection)*

Opposite: This 1908 advertisement appeared seven years after the department store was founded by E.L. Ward, who came from Essex. He took over a shop in the High Street called Stranger's and, with its name changed, the new retail outlet boasted epic opening hours typical of the time: 8 a.m. until 9 p.m. Mondays to Fridays and 8 a.m. until 11 p.m. on Saturdays. By 1910, twenty staff were employed. The business prospered and adjacent premises were acquired as they became available until by the time Ward's celebrated its fiftieth anniversary in 1951 over 100 staff were employed in twenty-six departments on three floors. E.L. Ward entered local politics, served twice as town mayor and was made an alderman. *(Author's collection)*

Alstone Spa, seen *c*. 1910, stood at the junction of Great Western Road and Millbrook Street. It opened in 1809 with a hexagonal pump room in the garden, but was too far out of town ever to be a resounding success with fashion-conscious tipplers. Townspeople who learned to swim at the Alstone baths, which were on the other side of the road, may recall that the former spa became a sweet shop. Pear drops or American hard gums helped restore flagging energy levels after all that doggy paddling. *(Joe Stevens)*

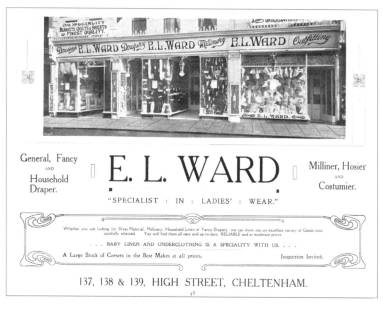

The good ladies of Highbury Congregational Church staged a sale of work in 1908 and were captured on film while doing so. What an exhibition of millinery the picture presents too. *(Gloucestershire Echo)*

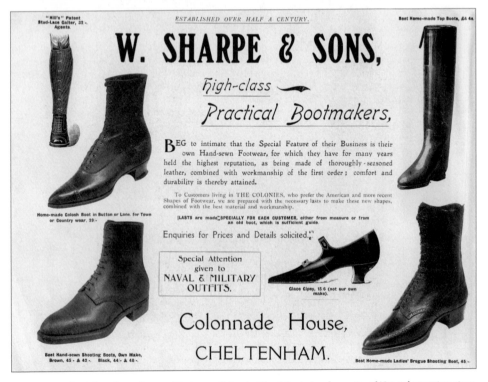

References in this Edwardian advert to 'Customers living in The Colonies' and promise of 'Special attention given to naval and military outfits' speak volumes about the clientèle in Cheltenham at the time. *(Author's collection)*

Peace & War

A curiosity in the shadow of Montpellier's Rotunda building is this fanciful statue of Edward VII, dressed in plus fours and Norfolk jacket, comforting an unknown waif. Unveiled on 10 October 1914, the unusual work was paid for by benefactors Mr and Mrs Drew who lived in Hatherley Court and devoted themselves to the rescue of old horses and seaside donkeys. *(Gloucestershire Echo)*

In 1912, the corporation declared a competition, inviting local architects to submit designs for new municipal offices up to a budget of £10,000. A site was set aside adjacent to the Winter Gardens and a prize of £100 was offered to the winning plan, with £50 for the runner-up. When the competition closing date arrived, all eight of the entries received were costed at more than £10,000. Consequently, the corporation rejected the lot. Four of the designs are shown here. Imagine how different the town centre would be if one of these monolithic structures now flanked Imperial Gardens on the Prom side . . . and you'll probably heave a sigh of relief that the project didn't happen. *(Gloucestershire Echo)*

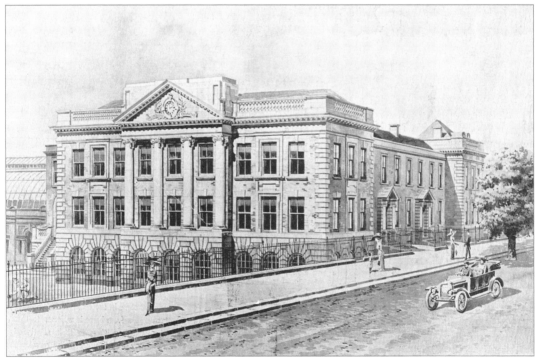

While war clouds were gathering over Europe, members of the Independent Order of Oddfellows, a secret fraternal benefit society founded in Manchester in 1813, were gathering in the Winter Gardens for a conference. This rare glimpse inside the great glasshouse reveals Ottoman-influenced decor, peppered with the pomp and pageantry of Britain at the peak of its imperial might. Facial hair was well represented as well. *(Gloucestershire Echo)*

The British chess championships were staged at the Town Hall in 1913, when players from all over the country arrived to follow their chequered careers. *The Gloucestershire Chronicle & Graphic* tells us that 'The whole of the catering for the conference was in the hands of the Oriental Café Company, High Street and the Promenade, Cheltenham, and gave the utmost satisfaction.' *(Gloucestershire Echo)*

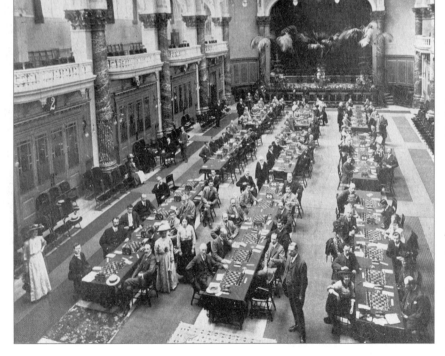

For the customer who was more concerned about style than economy, Vanderplank was the preferred choice of fashion-conscious women in the second decade of the twentieth century. This High Street costumier and furrier was noted for its exclusive prices and exotic window displays, which at one time featured a brace of stuffed capercaillie. New showrooms opened in 1914 with the convoluted promise that 'Blouses, Dainty and Useful, ever a fascination to the fair sex, with Millinery that is correct, are the Centre of Attraction in these Rooms'. *(Gloucestershire Echo)*

This First World War picture shows the High Street at its junction with North Street to the left and the Colonnade to the right. Before the building that was home to Dodwell & Sons, the stationers, was demolished to make way for the traffic roundabout, this quarter of the town centre was quite different in character. *(Peter Stephens)*

A car and a motorcycle combination feature among the mostly horse-drawn traffic in this view of the Promenade. Shops on the far side are, from left to right, James & Sons Chemists, G.H. Bayley & Sons house agents and auctioneers and Gordon Baynton fabric supplies. *(Peter Stephens)*

Pittville Gates, seen here *c.* 1910, announced the entrance to Joseph Pitt's grand estate. Late in the nineteenth century the town council commissioned Letherens iron foundry at Sunningend (now Lansdown Industrial Estate) to make the arch that can be seen spanning the central pillars in this picture. *(Peter Stephens)*

Flat-capped and aproned shop staff stand proudly before a display of hares and wares that then made customers salivate with anticipation – and today would have public health inspectors dry mouthed with disbelief. From 1952 until his death in 1989, this shop was the chock-a-block Aladdin's cave owned by eccentric antiques collector Ron Summerfield. Over the years he filled the shop and the rooms above, plus a large house in Bayshill Road and a barn in Derbyshire, with pictures, porcelain, furniture, knick-knackery – in fact whatever caught his eye. But rarely would he sell anything. Many of his treasures can be seen in Cheltenham's Art Gallery and Museum. *(Author's collection)*

When the west wing of Arle Court was set ablaze in February 1914 *the Gloucestershire Graphic* recorded: 'Despite the tempestuous weather, the inmates had to escape hurriedly in their night attire, three of the servants jumping from their bedroom window. One of them broke her arm and another injured her spine.' At the time of the fire Arle Court was owned by Herbert Unwin, a wealthy local businessman. George Dowty bought the house plus eight cottages and 100 acres for £6,000 in 1935. In the 1990s the building became Cheltenham Film Studios. *(Gloucestershire Echo)*

H.E. Steel Ltd styled itself 'The leading motor firm of the county' with 'The most modern and complete garages in the Midlands'. At this time if you wanted a new motor car and could afford the luxury you didn't pop along to your local showroom and buy a model off the shelf. Instead you chose the chassis, then specified the style of bodywork and interior of your choice. This done, skilled coachbuilders set to work and the conveyance you ordered would be finished some weeks later. Individual production was the norm. Mass production was an American invention not yet imported. *(Author's collection)*

News that Cheltenham-born Edward Wilson had died with Captain Scott in Antarctica reached the town in February 1913. A fund was immediately set up to provide a monument and the original plan was that two plaques – one for Scott, the other for Wilson – should be cast and hung in the Town Hall. Wilson's widow intervened, however. She said that her husband, as a lifelong nature lover, had always preferred to be outside. So instead of Town Hall plaques, a bronze statue – modelled by Captain Scott's widow Kathleen – was commissioned and placed on a plinth made by the local firm of R.L. Boulton & Sons in the Promenade's Long Garden. It was unveiled by Sir Clarence Markham – Arctic explorer and president of the Royal Geographical Society – on 9 July 1914. *(Gloucestershire Echo)*

These five shop assistants from Cavendish House, seen with Sergeant-Major Wilson of the Cheltenham recruiting office, were among the first volunteers to join up in August 1914. Another of the earliest recruits was 33-year-old Edwin Willoughby, editor of the *Gloucestershire Echo*. He was killed a year later, leading his company into action at Gallipoli. *(Gloucestershire Echo)*

Cheltenham, like most towns and cities throughout the country, was gripped by jingoistic euphoria. Recruitment rallies, such as those staged in the Town Hall and the Territorial Army Drill Hall in North Street, drew eager crowds. Throngs surged to open-air meetings at the Prom end of Clarence Street – and by October 1914 over 1,400 locals had signed up. *(Gloucestershire Echo)*

The cyclist section of E Company (Cheltenham) of the 5th Battalion the Gloucester Regiment. *(Gloucestershire Echo)*

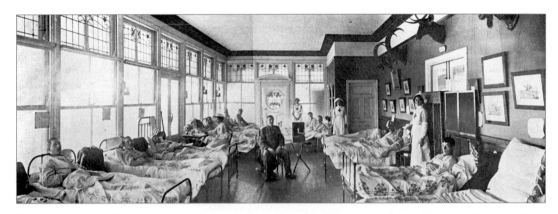

The racecourse opened as a 100-bed hospital, receiving its first influx of wounded Belgian soldiers on 28 October 1914. It was one of eight Voluntary Aid Detachment (VAD) hospitals established in Cheltenham, almost all of them in buildings that still stand. A fully equipped operating theatre was located at Prestbury Park, complete with electric lighting installed in June 1914. Belgian, British, Canadian and French casualties from the trenches were ferried by ship to Southampton, then on to Cheltenham aboard special trains. *(Gloucestershire Echo)*

The Priory, London Road, became a hospital in 1916 and was paid for by public subscription. The town's VAD hospitals did a fine job. They were well organised and coped efficiently with a huge workload; what's more, the standard of care must have been high as only a small percentage of patients failed to recover. All this sterling work was carried out by volunteers – not just the nursing staff, but also those who ran the war hospital supply depot, which was at 28 Imperial Gardens. *(Peter Stephens)*

Between the Wars

The Long Garden in the rain, early 1930s. Despite post-war depression, car ownership boomed in the '20s. The Austin 7, introduced in 1922, brought motoring within the price range of Mr and Mrs Average. Then in 1930, the Morris Minor (there are two examples in this picture, one behind the other outside the YMCA on the right) continued the theme when it became the first British car to sell for as little as £100. As we can see, cars then were black, or black. (*Author's collection*)

The pinnacled tower of Holy Trinity in Portland Street rises from the centre of this aerial view, *c.* 1930. In the left foreground is St Margaret's, a grand, early nineteenth-century house with grounds that became the Black & White coach station in 1932. Passengers bound for all parts of the country bought tickets in the converted St Margaret's house until December 1940, when a Luftwaffe bomb destroyed the building. *(Peter Stephens)*

The Black & White company was founded in 1926 to provide a regular road service between Cheltenham and the capital, plus pleasure tours of the county and the Cotswolds. When the firm became part of Associated Motorways, Cheltenham was established as the hub of a rapidly expanding national coach network. During the 1930s, a day trip to Weston-super-Mare by Black & White coach was priced at 7s 6d. *(Gloucestershire Echo)*

The Prom in sunshine, early 1930s. The lamp standard in the centre foreground was a 'tall twin'. Cast in Worcester and decorated about the base with Cheltenham's coat of arms, these appeared in pairs either side of the Prom with a single electric orb suspended between them. This arrangement was made necessary by the dense foliage of the Prom's trees. *(Author's collection)*

A white-gloved policeman waves on an open-topped touring car approaching from Lansdown Road in this 1929 view. Behind him is the Gordon lamp. In 1885 residents at Montpellier thought an ornamental lamp might brighten up the area. When General Gordon was killed at Khartoum later that year, the residents decided their lamp – a grand affair with base of red granite, stem of cast-iron and a halo of three gas orbs – should be erected in the military man's memory. A public appeal for funds was made and £20 trickled in. As the light cost £200 the organisers had to make up the difference. *(Peter Stephens)*

Lilleybrook Hotel opened in 1922. Before that the house, which dates from 1848, had been home to a family named Lord. *(Joe Stevens)*

The Queen's Hotel, seen here *c.* 1930, was built in 1837 – opening a year later at a cost of £47,000. Over the years the Queen's has been temporary home to a glittering array of notables including Prince Louis Jerome Napoleon, the Rajah of Sarawak and the Prince of Wales, later Edward VII. Bob Hope was among the celebrities who visited during the Second World War when the American Services Club took up residence. *(Author's collection)*

It's the late 1920s and we're in the Cadena Café on the corner of Imperial Lane and the Prom. In this fashionable meeting place, black-frocked, frilly-pinnied waitresses fetched and carried. The premises opened in 1906 as the Cosy Corner tea rooms, owned by a catering firm called the Oriental Café Company. In 1923 the name changed to Cadena and there was a second branch in the High Street near the Rodney Road junction. Today the building is Habitat. *(Author's collection)*

The ordinary had haircuts, the discerning went to Foice's. At least that was how Cheltenham's most up-market crimper billed itself. According to an advert from 1926, when these photographs were taken, this was no mere hairdresser's, but 'a series of charming salons in which artists express their art'. Mr F.J. Foice – a member of the International Hairdressing Academy of London – left Kensington for Cheltenham in 1901. In July of that year he acquired premises at 20 The Promenade, which had previously been occupied by a tailoring business. A major refurbishment marked the firm's twenty-fifth anniversary, by which time Foice & Co. employed a staff of twenty-five. *(Joan Ashton)*

On Foice's top floor was the postiche department, where up to forty women workers at a time ruined their eyesight making wigs from human hair. This testing task involved knotting single strands through tiny gauge gauze, but it was good business. The hair was usually provided by people without much who were happy to be paid little for their locks, while the wigs were sold to those with a great deal who didn't mind paying through the nose. *(Joan Ashton)*

43

Stanley Baldwin peers from a poster (there he is to the right of the Marmite) adjacent to Fred^k Wright's tobacconist's shop on the corner of Ambrose Street, which suggests this photo was taken at the time of the 1929 election. Fred^k Wright's first shop opened in the Colonnade in 1839 and the firm had another town premises in the High Street, plus branches further afield in Gloucester, Hereford, Worcester, Tewkesbury, Stroud, Malvern and Bath. *(Author's collection)*

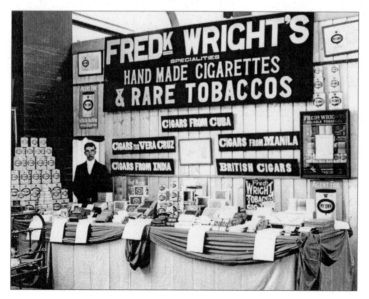

Fred^k Wright's stand at a trade show in the Winter Gardens, *c.* 1920. Incidentally, cigarettes were made in Cheltenham during the 1920s. The factory stood at the junction of Bath Road with Vernon Place in a building that later became Tilley's Crumpet factory and is now a night club. Ciggies sold under the 'X-Service' brand name and came in pink packets that featured the motif of a First World War soldier in trenchcoat, well lumbered with his accoutrements. *(Author's collection)*

This photo from the 1939 *Cheltenham Chronicle & Graphic* captures William Candy, by trade a china rivetter, at his premises in Sherborne Place (It looks as though Tabby never went short of a meal). *(Gloucestershire Echo)*

Pile it high was plainly the preferred style of window presentation at A.V.C. Paynter's general store seen here in about 1920. It stood in the High Street, looking up St George's Street. The advertising bills in the window of Martin's, the wine merchant to the left, are evocative of their time. One urges passers-by to 'Come in and buy a bottle of Wincarnis'. *(Author's collection)*

This 1932 photograph of a man with his legs and arms in buckets, apparently plugged into the mains electricity supply, was used to advertise the Cheltenham Spa Medical Baths. This hydro clinic peddled treatments for almost all known ailments, by the application externally and internally of the town's efficacious, saline waters. It is recorded that some eighty borings were made before spa water of the required quality for the medical baths was found at the junction of Bath Road and Oriel Road. The rooms in which the baths were housed are today part of the Playhouse theatre. *(Gloucestershire Echo)*

Bradley Road, Charlton Kings, was the only completed section of a bypass planned for Cheltenham in the 1930s. Looking up Cirencester Road we can see the New Inn, now called the Little Owl. Further up the road, Charlton Kings railway station was found on the right from where an engineering firm operates today. Bradley Road was named after its builders, Bradley's of Swindon. *(Joe Stevens)*

Cheltenham College, Bath Road, 1920. The building dates from the time of the school's foundation in the 1840s and was designed by Bath architect James Wilson. *(Peter Stephens)*

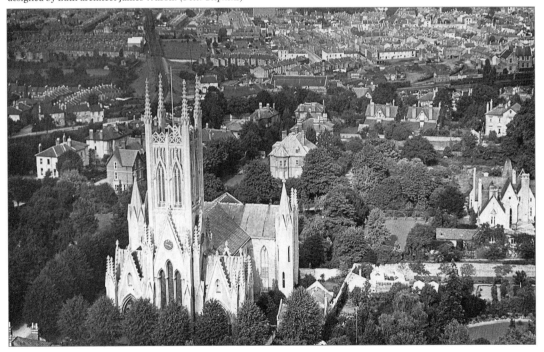

Splendidly Gothic Christ Church looms to the fore in this aerial view of the 1930s. The original design by the local architects R. and C. Jearrad was embellished by others, there were problems with the builders, the project ran well over budget . . . but for all that the result is a spectacular building. *(Peter Stephens)*

This 1930s photo shows Highbury Congregational Church in Winchcombe Street shortly before it closed. An application was made by the Gaumont-British Picture Corporation to demolish this town centre landmark and replace the building with a cinema. Uproar! Replace a House of God with a palace of Mammon? Out with the rood screen and in with the silver screen? Hollywood in place of Holy Scriptures? Despite the outcry, the Odeon has occupied the site ever since. *(Joe Stevens)*

In this postcard franked 1928, tram tracks in Ambrose Street guide the eye towards the magnificent spire of St Gregory's, which dates from 1854. The architect was Charles Hansom of Bristol. *(Author's collection)*

In 1938 Cambray aperient, saline and chalybeate spa pump room was demolished. The octagonal Gothic fancy stood on the corner of Oriel Road and Rodney Road (now Rodney Road car park) and opened for business in 1834. (*Author's collection*)

More than just a cinema, the Regal (later the ABC-Regal, then the ABC) in Cheltenham's Promenade was a gateway to the glamour of the movies. The fantasy began the moment you crossed the threshold and entered the foyer, from which rose a sweeping staircase that might have been plucked from a Busby Berkeley production. It was the work of well-known cinema architects W.R. Glen and L.C. Norton and opened for business on 2 January 1939. With its seating capacity of 1,165 downstairs and 674 upstairs, Cheltenham's Regal was the largest cinema on the EMI circuit in the country. The longest-serving member of staff was Rose Peters, who lived in Baker Street and was a cleaner at the cinema from February 1939 until its closure on Saturday 14 November 1981. (*Gloucestershire Echo*)

The Second World War

On 1 September 1939 the first consignment of wartime evacuees arrived in Cheltenham. The mayor was at Lansdown station to welcome 267 schoolchildren from Birmingham. Half a dozen double-deckers drove the children to Naunton Park school, where they were billeted to homes in Leckhampton. Within a few days the influx of evacuees from the Midlands had increased Cheltenham's population by 2,000. *(Gloucestershire Echo)*

Boots roundabout in the early months of the Second World War. On one side of Charles Dickens' tobacconists is the town clock, on the other a sign for the Army Recruitment Office. *(Peter Stephens)*

Boots Corner in the early months of the war again, but looking from the opposite direction. On top of Shirers & Lances, seen to the right of the picture, an air-raid siren was positioned, while in the basement of this department store the headquarters of the ARP (Air Raid Precautions) were established. *(Peter Stephens)*

Trench bomb shelters, like this one at St Paul's, were dug in the grounds of all local schools. At the boys' grammar school, which then stood in the High Street, the central corridor was shored up with sturdy timbers to form a makeshift shelter. *(Gloucestershire Echo)*

Children from St Paul's infants' school practising gas mask drill as they enter their bombproof shelter, 1939. By the end of August 49,000 gas masks had been distributed to households in Cheltenham, but due to administrative error nobody in Whaddon received one. More masks were ordered, but Whaddon's residents went without until some time after war was declared on 3 September. *(Gloucestershire Echo)*

Shelters capable of accommodating 7,000 people in total were also constructed in the town centre. The largest – a trench with shored-up sides, timber and corrugated iron roof, covered over with earth – was in Imperial Gardens. Others stood at the athletic ground, Royal Crescent and in the North Street car park of the Liberal Club. Smaller, brick-walled, concrete-roofed shelters were dotted about all over town. There was also one in Clarence Parade, outside the *Echo* offices. *(Gloucestershire Echo)*

'Scrap for Spitfires' was the slogan – and local people contributed aluminium pots and pans by the thousand to be recycled for the war effort. *(Gloucestershire Echo)*

An inspection of the Cheltenham and District LDV (Local Defence Volunteers), Cheltenham College, July 1940. After the evacuation of British and French troops from Dunkirk between 27 May and 4 June 1940, fears that Germany would soon invade Britain seemed well founded. The LDV, later renamed the Home Guard, was rapidly formed in response to the threat. *(Gloucestershire Echo)*

A Matilda tank in manoeuvres with the LDV at Aggs Hill, 14 October 1941. *(Gloucestershire Echo)*

Cheltenham Services Club opened in a former riding school in Regent Street on 5 November 1943. It was the brainchild of local benefactor Cyril Bird of Treaford, Lansdown Road, whose mission was to provide a venue that would contribute 'to the moral welfare of Cheltenham, as well as to the pleasure and well-being of the forces'. Within three months of opening the club had 3,000 members – Brits, Poles, Latvians, Lithuanians, Norwegians, New Zealanders, Australians . . . And when Uncle Sam turned Cheltenham into a supply centre in preparation for D-day, GIs by the train, truck and Jeep load introduced jazz and razzmatazz to the club's usual fare of table tennis and iced buns. The club closed with a final tea dance in 1946. (*Gloucestershire Echo*)

Opposite, top: Cheltenham suffered its worst night of bombing on Wednesday 11 December 1940, when 600 people were made homeless. At 7.20 p.m. siting flares were dropped over the town and ten minutes later incendiary, high-explosive and oil bombs fell – over 100 in total. The fronts of four houses collapsed in Kipling Road when a bomb impacted between Shelley and Spencer Roads, leaving a large crater. (*Gloucestershire Echo*)

Opposite, bottom: Someone who must have thought himself the luckiest man alive that night was Cyril Price, who incidentally played cricket for Cheltenham. Cyril was watching the dramatic events from Pilley railway bridge in Old Bath Road when a bomb fell on it, passed clean through and exploded on the line below. A wooden footway for pedestrians was placed over the hole where Pilley bridge had been – locals crossing it referred to 'walking the plank'. Pilley had the distinction of being the last war-damaged bridge in the country to be repaired. A long argument raged about who was responsible for meeting the cost of reconstruction before it finally reopened in 1954. (*Gloucestershire Echo*)

Half Stoneville Street was demolished on 11 December 1940 when a large bomb landed on the railway embankment nearby. Ten people were killed, some of them children. On the other side of Gloucester Road a gas holder was hit. *(Gloucestershire Echo)*

On that fateful night in 1940 a bomb fell on this house in Montpellier Villas where three people died, plus other homes in Parabola Road, Christchurch Road, Lansdown Road, Merrivale Gardens . . . *(Gloucestershire Echo)*

. . . and
Suffolk Road.
(Gloucestershire Echo)

St Paul's College
in Swindon
Road narrowly
escaped in July
1942 when a
bomb exploded,
leaving a large
crater near
the entrance.
*(Gloucestershire
Echo)*

Brunswick Street was hit on 27 July 1942 . . .
(Gloucestershire Echo)

. . . but by first light, when gangs of volunteers
and service people set to the formidable task of
clearing up, Union Jacks fluttered defiantly from
the debris . . . *(Gloucestershire Echo)*

. . . and the Women's Volunteer Service tea van
helped to keep spirits up. *(Gloucestershire Echo)*

George Dowty standing by a test rig for the Lancaster bomber's undercarriage. During the war Dowty's supplied a total of 87,000 undercarriages, almost a quarter of them for Lancasters. *(Author's collection)*

The war over at last, everyday life began to return to Cheltenham. In 1945, the Borough Council decided to convert the Montpellier Baths in Bath Road into the Civic Playhouse theatre. The first production staged was *Arms and the Man*, by George Bernard Shaw. *(Gloucestershire Echo)*

High Street, looking towards the Strand, late 1940s. Petrol rationing continued, which meant cars were few and far between. *(Peter Stephens)*

Late 1940s in the Prom, where the wartime standing water tanks have been removed and the flower bed outside the central post office replanted. 'We are here for four days. Hope to go over some of the old haunts we visited during the war', reads the message on this postcard. *(Peter Stephens)*

The 1950s

In 1952 H.H. Martyn & Co. cast the Commando Memorial, seen being worked on here. The bronze stands at Spean Bridge, Fort William, and commemorates the 35,000 officers and commandos who were trained in Scotland during the Second World War. On scaffolding to the left is Bill Tovey and right Bill Anderson. On the floor is the artist Scott Sutherland of the Dundee School of Art who designed the piece. He stayed with Bill Tovey at his home in Naunton Park while the work was being completed. (*Jean Hewitt*)

The finished memorial at Sunningend (now Lansdown Industrial Estate). Each of the figures is 9ft tall, in full battle dress, rifles slung across shoulders. It took twelve months to complete in Martyn's foundry and was unveiled by the Queen Mother on 27 September 1952. The Cheltenham firm didn't put its mark on many of the pieces that were cast, but stamped into the base of the Commando Monument are the words 'H.H. Martyn. Cheltenham'. (*Jean Hewitt*)

A statue of Robert the Bruce in full armour on horseback was created by the artist Charles d'O. Pilkington Jackson, who fashioned the entire model in clay. At Sunningend plaster casts were taken from the original and cut so that casting could be undertaken in sections – probably dozens of separate sections for a piece this size. When the bronze castings came out of the kiln they were finished ('chased') by hand, then treated with acids and powders to produce the patina and colours required by the artist. Lastly the individual sections were welded together and after some final chasing the piece was ready for despatch. (*Jean Hewitt*)

Some 4 tons of bronze were used in the Robert the Bruce piece, which cost £27,000 and stands today at Bannockburn. A second casting can be seen in Calgary, Alberta, where it commemorates the thousands of Scots who moved to make a new life in Canada. (*Jean Hewitt*)

Few names conjure the romantic era of transatlantic ocean travel as irresistibly as the RMS *Queen Elizabeth*. The 1950s were the Cunarder's heyday. The world's largest liner, a palace that plied the seas, a wonder of the modern world, the Queen Elizabeth provided an international shop window for British craftsmanship, much of which was produced in Cheltenham by H.H. Martyn & Co. (*Author's collection*)

Fitting out ocean liners was no novelty for the Sunningend firm. Its craftsmen contributed to the opulence of many of the world's most famous ships including the *Empress of Britain*, the *Queen Mary*, the *Canberra*, the *Lusitania*, the *Queen Elizabeth II* and the ill-fated *Titanic*. Contracts for the *Queen Elizabeth* mostly involved Martyn's metalwork and decorative plaster departments. Here we see the great ship's library. *(Author's collection)*

The Smoking Room on the *Queen Elizabeth*, 1958. For those with a taste for the technical, the ship was 1,031ft long by 118ft at her widest point and 234ft from keel to masthead with a draught of just over 39ft. Power was provided by steam turbines, which propelled her 83,673 gross tonnage through the water. There were 13 decks connected by 34 lifts for the 2,240 passengers to explore and 1,318 officers and crew to keep ship-shape. *(Author's collection)*

Corporation roadroller JAA 643 at work on the new Princess Elizabeth Way, looking from the junction with Dormer Road, October 1951. Coronation Square and Princess Elizabeth Way are names that hint heavily at the time when Cheltenham's largest housing estate was built. Started in the early 1950s, around 3,000 new homes had appeared at Hesters Way by the end of the decade, a continuation of the council's housing programme, which had been interrupted by the war. *(Author's collection)*

Hesters Way meets St Marks, January 1953. Here we see Wasley Road (named after Si Wasley who sold the land) prior to development, with Kipling Road in the background. If you've ever wondered where the name Hester came from, the title can be traced back to 1334. In that year a survey of the manor of Cheltenham records a tenant William Herte – and over the years the land that was Herte's became Hesters. *(Author's collection)*

A tarmacked cul-de-sac at Hesters Way, awaiting the arrival of its houses, 1951. Redgrove Road perhaps? *(Author's collection)*

A splendid Rolls-Royce fills up at Hall's garage in this early 1950s scene at the junction of Lansdown Road and Gloucester Road. Just beyond the filling station is the Lansdown Inn (the site is now occupied by TGI Fridays), while on the other side of the road, partly obscured by a traffic bollard, we can see a drinking fountain and horse trough. In the right foreground is Lansdown Castle, a Victorian Gothic house with a castellated roof dating from the 1850s. In about 1870 the building became a grocery shop and that's how it remained until it was demolished in the early 1970s. *(Author's collection)*

St James's station, shortly before the broach spire of St Matthew's Church (to the right of St Gregory's in the photograph) was removed for reasons of safety in 1952. St James's was the grandest of Cheltenham's stations and stood on land that was formerly Jessop's pleasure gardens. It was from this terminus with its cobbled approach and impressive portico that the famous 'Cheltenham Flyer' began its journey to London. *(Joe Stevens)*

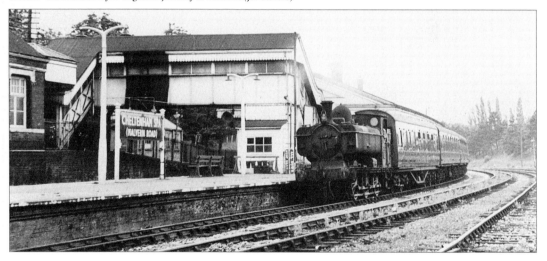

In 1908, the GWR opened Malvern Road station, with its curving main platform 700ft in length, to serve the new Honeybourne line. The development meant demolishing 70 houses in Great Western Road, Bloomsbury Place, Carlton Place, Hill View Cottages, Marsh Cottages and Whitehall Street. A pub named the Cherry Tree was knocked down too. The new line also cut through the old town cemetery and 300 bodies had to be removed to another resting place. During the First World War Malvern Road station closed. It opened again in 1919 and in 1925 was renamed Cheltenham Spa. *(Joe Stevens)*

Local people of ripening years may remember browsing or buying at Tinkler's in the Lower High Street. A sixteenth-century building, the shop was an Aladdin's cave of baskets and buckets, dusters and dustbins – and all those 1950s brand-named goods that ended in 'o' such as Brasso, Rinso, Omo, Brillo . . . Tinkler's fell to the hammer in 1967. Its site is now the entrance to the car park that runs through to Swindon Road. *(Joe Stevens)*

The Jensen 541 car parked outside the Restoration Inn on the corner of the High Street and Grosvenor Street dates this view to about 1956. Besides its wholesale drinks business, Dobell's owned pubs in Cheltenham, Newport (Monmouthshire) and Tewkesbury. *(Joe Stevens)*

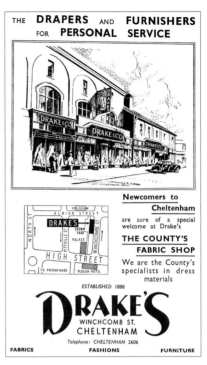

Drake's of Winchcombe Street (or Winchcomb as it appears in this 1950 advert) was founded in 1888 and remained in business for the following ninety years. At first a drapery store, Drake's branched into home fabrics, upholstery and furniture. In the 1920s and '30s the shop pioneered the presentation of bedroom and lounge suites in room displays, so customers could see what that armchair looked like alongside this coffee table. Sounds simple now, but it was quite a breakthrough at the time. The shop boasted an impressive sign – protruding from the wall like a pub's – depicting the *Golden Hind*, an oblique reference to Drake. *(Author's collection)*

The Long Garden, looking towards the cenotaph, 1955. The original design for this war memorial by R.L. Boulton & Sons, of Bath Road, was for a gold-topped obelisk on a stone base in black marble covered by a canopy supported on four classical pillars – estimated price £3,500. An appeal was launched, but raised only £1,150, so Boulton's was asked for a budget-priced version. The result is the 24ft-high simple cenotaph that stands in the Prom today. *(Author's collection)*

71

The most striking feature of Montpellier – then as now – was the Rotunda. But when this photograph was taken in the mid-1950s this great tureen over the spa that J.B. Papworth designed in 1825 was in a perilous condition. Lloyd's Bank bought the building for £14,000 in 1961 and a survey revealed that the 160ft-diameter, 60ft-high dome had dropped 3in and was sagging on rotted roof beams. Two tons of copper and another two of lead were removed in the restoration, along with more tons of ornate plaster. The number of cars in this view suggests it was taken after February 1953 when branded fuel was reintroduced and wartime rationing restrictions lifted. *(Peter Stephens)*

Moray House Hotel

Two minutes from Promenade and Shops   *Telephone:* Cheltenham 53613
LICENSED

A.A.   PARABOLA ROAD   R.A.C.

QUIET .. CENTRAL .. SOUTH ASPECT

40 Bedrooms (ten on Hall-Floor) with "Somnus" Beds
Hot and Cold running water, gas or electric fires and
telephones

CENTRAL HEATING

Spacious Comfortable Lounge, Writing Rooms, etc.
Dining-room to seat 150 open to non-residents

Wedding Receptions, Bridge Teas, Private Parties catered for

REALLY GOOD FOOD   ..   OWN FARM PRODUCE
LOCK-UP GARAGES   ..   ATTRACTIVE GARDEN

Moray House Hotel, Parabola Road, which by 1950 when this advert appeared had probably recovered from its wartime role as a servicemen's club. During the war Norman Wisdom was stationed in Cheltenham with the Signals Corps and lived with his wife in a flat over a Bath Road shop. In his autobiography *Don't Laugh at Me* (published in 1992 by Arrow Books), the versatile clown recalls attending dances at the Moray House, which was later renamed the Carlton Hotel. *(Author's collection)*

It's a sad reflection on the British motor-cycle industry that of the marques listed in this mid-1950s advert only Triumph is in business today (and that's a different company). A. Williams founded the firm in 1904 and his son Jack – dubbed the Cheltenham Flyer – was a star rider of his time. A works rider for Norton, Jack competed in trials, grass-track racing, hill climbs, scrambles, road racing, played motorcycle football for Cheltenham and gained a national reputation by scoring successes in such events as the Lancashire Grand National and the Scott Trial. *(Author's collection)*

Traffic passes either way along the Prom in this early '50s scene. On the corner of Imperial Lane is Dale, Forty & Co, which sold sheet music, records and musical instruments. Many who were children at the time will recall practising at home on a recorder bought or hired from the shop. Their parents will remember the sound with pleasure. *(Peter Stephens)*

On their way to Hatherley school in the 1950s, these children cross the narrow railway bridge in Hatherley Lane. Steam hangs in the air from a locomotive chuffing towards Churchdown and Inspector Maigret passes in his Citroën Traction Avant. Shortly after diesel had superseded steam, the bridge was replaced and the school closed. *(Author's collection)*

This picture postcard is franked 6 April 1951 and cost 2*d* to send. (It was from Ann to her Auntie Grace in Bournemouth.) Buildings at the east end of the Colonnade were pulled down in the late '30s to make way for the traffic island, which is considered by many to be the centre of Cheltenham. It's curious that a town with so many distinguished architectural features should have a roundabout at its heart. *(Peter Stephens)*

The 1960s

This biggest swinger in 1960s Cheltenham was the demolition man's hammer. A landmark building that bit the dust in 1967 was St John's Church, which stood where Albion Street curves into Berkeley Street. St John's was designed by J.B. Papworth, the distinguished architect responsible for much of Lansdown and Montpellier. It was consecrated in 1829 and one of its incumbents – the Revd Valpy French – went on to become Bishop of Lahore. *(Joe Stevens)*

Winchcombe Street from the High Street end, seen here shortly before demolition of the east side began in 1962 to make way for the less than lovely concrete terrace that squats on the spot today. Swept away was the Cake Basket café, Peacocks (many local kids spent their first day at school in an Airtex vest from Peacocks) with its a glass roof – and almost everything you can see in the picture. (*Gloucestershire Echo*)

Winchcombe Street from the Albion Street end, captured at the same time as the picture above. The premises in the right foreground (it's now A Plan Insurance) were a saddlery called Stephens & Son, which also sold travel trunks and suitcases. Nearby stood Bastin's electrical shop. (*Gloucestershire Echo*)

Prior to demolition, buildings on the east side of Winchcombe Street had fallen into disrepair, as this view taken from the lane to the rear on 26 January 1962 reveals. *(Author's collection)*

Winchcombe Street, west side, February 1961. The large white building was Humphrey's Horse Repository and Carriage Showrooms, established 1818. Some time after this picture was taken it became an indoor market and the façade remains to this day. A. Maher's barber shop and the Avery Scales office were knocked down as part of a road improvement scheme. *(Author's collection)*

The inner ring road today passes over the spot in North Place where North House and A.A. Motors stood when photographed on St Valentine's day, 1961. On the extreme left of the picture is the building that's now home to the Storyteller restaurant. *(Author's collection)*

We're looking from St Mary's parish churchyard towards Well Walk in the late 1960s, when the Cheltenham & Gloucester Building Society acquired the former warehouse of Shirers & Lances department store. The building dated from 1861, but was pulled down in 1974 to make way for the C & G's enlarged HQ in Clarence Street. *(Gloucestershire Echo)*

The United Demolition signboard stands outside the boys' grammar school in the High Street, heralding its imminent demise in 1967. The building dated from 1889 and was designed by local architects Knight and Chatters. All the tricks of the Tudor Gothic style were showcased in its façade with buttresses, stone-mullioned windows, gargoyles, heraldic decorations, steep gables, a castellated roofline and even an octagonal turret that might have been plucked from a Walt Disney fantasy. Inside, though, the school was a bit gloomy. *(Joe Stevens)*

The Rolling Stones were riding a peak of popularity when they came to Cheltenham's Odeon to play two sell-out concerts on Thursday 10 September 1964. Fans laid a special claim on the Stones, because Brian Jones (fourth from left) was a local lad and a former pupil of the boys' grammar school. He died in July 1969 and in an obituary Dr Arthur Bell, headmaster, wrote 'Brian Jones seemed to me to be essentially a sensitive and vulnerable boy, not at all cut out for the rough and tumble of the commercial world.' *(Gloucestershire Echo)*

Cheltenham (Lansdown) 1965
Platform extension works in progress
C BH Swallow 055

COACH OUTING   BLACK & WHITE MOTORWAYS LTD.   SAVINGS CARD

As all the other railway stations in town were closed in the mid-1960s, courtesy of Dr Beeching, Lansdown had to be enlarged. Here we see the platform being extended in 1965. Lansdown was Cheltenham's first station when it opened in June 1840 and was designed by Samuel Daukes, the architect responsible for St Paul's training college and St Peter's Church. *(Peter Stephens)*

Never one to miss a promotional trick, the Black & White ran a savings club in the '60s. Members paid by instalment until they had put by enough for a trip, perhaps to London – in those pre-motorway days a major expedition. First stop out from Cheltenham along the meandering A40 was Northleach, then Burford, Witney and Oxford, where everyone got off to stretch their legs, eat packed lunches and slurp from a Thermos. Then it was on to London Victoria. *(Joe Stevens)*

The Majestic Hotel, pictured here in the early '60s, stood on the corner of Park Place and Ashford Road. It opened in 1932, then after a rebuilding programme was officially opened again by the Mayor, E.L. Ward (owner of the High Street department store), in May 1934. A popular meeting place at the time, the bar was a curving sweep of light oak with chromium strips. Uplighters forced smudges of illumination to the ceiling and there was a ritzy white piano in the corner – like a set from *The Maltese Falcon*. The Majestic, known by then as the Park Place Hotel, was reduced to rubble in the 1980s and flats stand now where it stood then. *(Peter Stephens)*

Montpellier Hotel – a building that dates from about 1838 – in Bath Road was bought by Eagle Star in 1965 and renamed Eagle Lodge. The tower block Eagle Star House was built on adjacent land and opened in October 1968. (*Eagle Star Archives*)

This was how the Promenade looked when John, Paul, George and Ringo took the Odeon stage – and the town – by storm on 1 November 1963. On the bill with the mop-topped Fab Four were the Rhythm & Blues Quartet,

the Vernons Girls, Frank Berry, the Brook Brothers, Peter Jay and the Jaywalkers, plus the Kestrels. After the gig, The Beatles stayed at the Savoy Hotel in Bayshill Road. *(Gloucestershire Echo)*

Pedestrians in the High Street had to pick their way between oncoming traffic from both directions in the mid-1960s. Topped by a triangle, the road sign outside the Midland Bank warns of the low bridge at the Gloucester Road end of the street – a precise '920 yards ahead'. Shops in view over in Clarence Street are Watsons home furnishings, Clarks shoes, W. Wright jewellery and Charles Dickins tobacconist. *(Author's collection)*

Pandas on parade. The Lansdown Road police HQ was built in 1966 and two years later blue and white Austin 1100 panda cars were introduced.
(Gloucestershire Constabulary)

Despite the introduction of panda cars, bobbies on bikes were still a familiar sight about town. Alf Willis, seen here in the workshop in 1969, was the man who maintained the pedal power fleet of 250 two-wheelers. *(Gloucestershire Constabulary)*

The 1970s

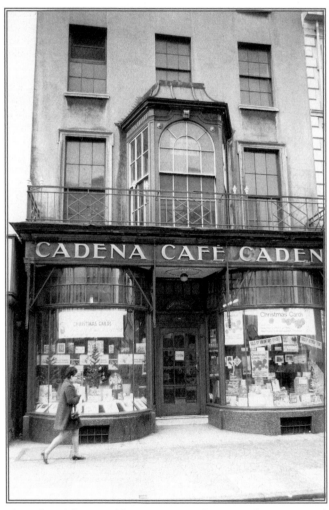

The Cadena Café, pictured here in 1970, stood at 126 High Street. Opened at the turn of the twentieth century, this was the first of two Cadenas. The second stood in the Promenade on the corner of Imperial Lane. *(Brian Donnan Photography)*

Skate was 3s 8d a pound at the High Street shop of fishmonger W. Dean & Sons when the camera clicked on this scene. The open-fronted premises displayed fishy wares on a slab of cold white marble, made the more chilly by liberal scatterings of crushed ice – flat, delicately spotted sole, eel-like huss and whelks struggling to climb out of their imprisoning bucket (every so often an assistant ran half a lemon round the rim to keep the molluscs in their place); whopping cod with bulging eyes; rosy-hued lobsters with pincers and whiskers and cooked prawns sold by the pint. *(Brian Donnan Photography)*

In 1970, this High Street location was redeveloped following a fire that gutted Tesco. Over the supermarket entrance a sign advertises Green Shield stamps, a popular dividend scheme for shoppers at the time. On the other side of Church Street is Hepworth's tailoring. *(Brian Donnan Photography)*

The Plough Hotel in Cheltenham's High Street, originally a coaching inn, was noted in the mid-eighteenth century as one of three in town that offered accommodation. To the rear was an extensive yard that served as a car park when this picture was taken in the early 1970s. The High Street entrance to the Regent Arcade now occupies the spot you see in the picture and the shopping mall covers ground that once rang to the clop of hoof and grind of wagon wheel when it was the coaching inn's yard. *(Brian Donnan Photography)*

On the far side of the High Street is the premises formerly occupied by Ward's department store, which had stood empty for three years when this picture was taken in the '70s. Nearer the camera is Charles Dickins tobacconist with its ornamental ironwork canopy. This was made by Charles Hancock – who worked for H.H. Martyn and later ran his own firm in Bennington Street – in about 1920. *(Brian Donnan Photography)*

The Coopers Arms on the corner of the High Street and Grosvenor Street seen in the early '70s. Its attractive tiled front looks Victorian, but is in fact later as the building suffered a serious fire between the wars. Notice the ceramic West Country Ales plaque above the entrance. Since the mid-1990s the pub has been called Cactus Jack's. *(Brian Donnan Photography)*

Pantie hose were down from 6s 11d to 5s 11d at Dorothy Perkins in 1970. The shop stood in the High Street opposite the Cambray junction. *(Brian Donnan Photography)*

The Famous has been in business from this site in the High Street since 1886. At that time its founder Edwin Cheeseright sold trousers at 13s and made-to-measure overcoats for 2 guineas. In 1896, the shop was bought by A.N. Cole and remains in the same family to this day. Thousands of Cheltenham children have started their school careers in a blazer from the Famous. *(Brian Donnan Photography)*

Seen here in the early '70s, the Lower High Street Ritz cinema opened in 1937 and was renamed the Essoldo in 1955, at which time it boasted the only CinemaScope screen in town. *Jason and the Golden Fleece* was the last film shown before closure in 1964 and conversion to the Legalite Casino Club – a bingo hall. *(Brian Donnan Photography)*

The Promenade suffered an architectural jolt in 1970 when the Quadrangle appeared at its junction with Oriel Road. A building called the New Club previously occupied the site, which was acquired by developers for £110,000. *(Brian Donnan Photography)*

Gloucestershire, Worcestershire and England cricketer Tom Graveney ran the Royal Oak in Prestbury during the 1970s. A fine and stylish batsman, Tom Graveney played in 79 tests and scored 4,482 runs including 11 centuries. He was awarded the OBE for services to cricket in 1968. *(Brian Donnan Photography)*

Arthur Negus, seen here at a Town Hall book fair in 1975, became everyone's favourite expert on antiques following his appearances in TV shows such as *Going for a Song* and *Antiques Roadshow*. A resident of Queen's Road, Arthur Negus's softly rounded Gloucestershire vowels and undisguised passion for a nicely turned leg assured his popularity. *(Brian Donnan Photography)*

The Holst Birthplace Museum opened in 1974 and was visited the following year by Imogen Holst, the composer's daughter. Cheltenham's most famous musical son – Gustav Theodore von Holst – earned himself pocket money as a student by playing trombone in a seaside band dressed as a Hungarian hussar. He also, of course, wrote *The Planets* and a galaxy of splendid music. *(Brian Donnan Photography)*

Michael Heseltine attended the Conservative Association's summer ball at Cheltenham Town Hall on 23 June 1977. Here we see him chatting to the faithful between quicksteps. *(Brian Donnan Photography)*

The St James's station site in 1970 with the town centre skyline punctuated by St Gregory's spire. The station closed in 1966. *(Brian Donnan Photography)*

In 1977 – the year in which the silver jubilee of Queen Elizabeth was celebrated – the Strand became Cheltenham's first pedestrianised area. At that time, out-of-town retail parks were still waiting to happen, so DIY and furniture stores such as Timberland were found in the High Street. *(Brian Donnan Photography)*

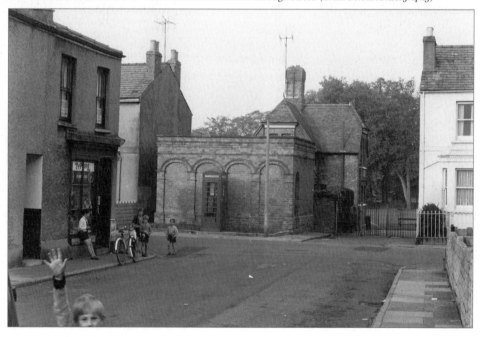

Another aspect of the retail revolution in recent decades has been the disappearance of corner shops – like this one at the junction of Brunswick Street and Marle Hill Road, St Paul's. The public conveniences on the opposite side of the road were demolished in the mid-1970s. *(Brian Donnan Photography)*

For a year or two in the mid-1970s this house stood in splendid isolation in the Portland Street/North Place car park awaiting the same fate as its neighbours. It brought to mind an Alfred Hitchcock film location. Looking beyond we can see the Black & White coach station and Whitbread tower block. *(Brian Donnan Photography)*

Cheltenham and County Cycling Club staged a Criterium in the town centre during May 1975. Here we see riders turning from the Prom to pass the Municipal Offices. The club was founded in 1921 and for a year or two operated as a section of the Harriers. Take a magnifying glass to that pay and display sign and you'll read that parking in the Long Garden was 2p an hour at the time. *(Brian Donnan Photography)*

Street parties, concerts, fireworks and silver jubilee celebrations of all kinds took place in town during the summer of 1977. Pittville Park was the venue for this display on 24 July. *(Brian Donnan Photography)*

Cheltenham Carnival, with the Granny's Folk Club float passing the Cotswold pub in Portland Street, 1975. Next door to the pub is the vacant premises previously occupied by Williams motorcycles. This building and its neighbour beyond were demolished to make way for the inner ring road. Granny's Folk Club, by the way, met at the Plough. *(Brian Donnan Photography)*

Another 1970s carnival, this time in the rain. We're looking from the corner of St George's Street down the Lower High Street. Fosters was a well-known clothes retailer for many years and (like the Famous) specialised in school uniforms. *(Brian Donnan Photography)*

The Salvation Army band marches along an unpedestrianised High Street in the mid-1970s. *(Brian Donnan Photography)*

In May 1977, Charles Irving, Conservative MP for the town, was given the Freedom of Cheltenham. Here the party of local dignitaries poses at the side entrance to the Town Hall. Centre front is Mayor Kirry Frewin with Charles Irving immediately to his rear. *(Brian Donnan Photography)*

The 1980s

Montpellier is a village within the town. It has its own scale, architecture and style, which by the 1980s was developing a distinctly continental flavour. Here we see a busy summer lunchtime with people at pavement tables outside the Rotunda pub. Charles Barnett's wet fish shop is nearer the camera, while the right side of the picture is framed by Montpellier Exchange. *(Brian Donnan Photography)*

For a few years Montpellier traders and residents joined forces to stage a summer fair. The setting was picturesque Montpellier Walk where properties are separated by Caryatids. There are thirty-two of these armless and doleful-looking ladies, based on classical Athenian statues. Two of their number date from 1840 and are made from terracotta, while the rest were copied locally – all except one, made of concrete and added in 1970. They're not all the same, by the way. Some have their left leg forward, some have their right leg forward – a classical version of the okey-cokey captured in stone. *(Brian Donnan Photography)*

Cricket on the lawn at Rosehill, a nineteenth-century house that was part of St Paul's teacher training college. Rosehill stood at Pittville at the junction of Evesham Road and New Barn Lane. It was demolished to make way for the office block that was at first occupied by Gulf Oil and is now home to UCAS (University College Admissions Services). *(Brian Donnan Photography)*

UCAS was previously called UCCA and when this photograph was taken in 1986 it occupied this unlovely block in Rodney Road. *(Brian Donnan Photography)*

This view from Imperial Lane looks across the Prom to the plot made vacant by the demolition of the ABC cinema, which closed on 14 November 1981 with a double bill of *Kentucky Fried Movie* and *The Other Cinderella*. The land was bought by developers for £400,000. *(Brian Donnan Photography)*

The former ABC cinema site showing work under way on the culvert through which the River Chelt flows. Royscot House was built here between 1985 and 1987 at a cost of £3 million and was designed by the Falconer Partnership of Stroud. *(Brian Donnan Photography)*

An early morning in June 1988 and a trio of street cleaners trundle their carts along Clarence Street from the depot in St James's Square. The Cheltenham & Gloucester Building Society HQ was built in the mid-1970s and the façade features a sculpture by Barbara Hepworth. The C & G left for Barnwood in 1990. *(Brian Donnan Photography)*

Glamour girl turned respected character actress Diana Dors (real name Diana Fluck) made a promotional visit to Cavendish House in February 1984. She's seen here in the Prom with the store's PR manager Pam Smiles and general manager Trevor Allinson. Dors died the following May. *(Brian Donnan Photography)*

The largest single development in Cheltenham during the 1980s was the Regent Arcade with its glass atrium, shown here. Costing £23 million, the shopping mall was built between 1982 and 1984 on the site of the 45-bedroomed Plough Hotel, its yard and car park. Considerable opposition to the scheme was voiced and 20,000 signatures were collected by people who didn't want the development at any price. Campaigners staged a photographic exhibition titled 'The Rape of Cheltenham' to illustrate how the town had suffered in the past at the hands of 'bureaucratic and speculative development at the expense of public opinion and sensible conservation values'. Despite the misgivings, the 185,000sqft arcade with its seventy-eight shops and parking for 540 cars was officially opened by the Princess Royal in May 1985. *(Brian Donnan Photography)*

Hatherley Brake stood at the junction of Hatherley Road and Hatherley Lane. In the 1930s it was a 'Garden school for backward children' as a bluntly worded advertisement tells us. Later the building became a Barnardo's home. It was demolished shortly after this photograph was taken in the early '80s and a development of houses occupies the spot today. *(Brian Donnan Photography)*

The Black & White coach station closed in 1986. This view (taken from the Whitbread tower) shows the extensive buildings, canopied area, garages and yard that fronted on St Margaret's Road. To the right, new buildings at the junction with North Place can be seen on the former Richard Pate's junior school site. *(Gloucestershire Echo)*

Madame Beatrix Taylor's splendid millinery establishment survived as Cheltenham's only specialist hat maker until the mid-1980s. The shop stood in the Strand adjacent to Skiff & Hawkins, a fashion shop that closed at about the same time. *(Brian Donnan Photography)*

Sandford Lido
1935 - 1985

In 1985 Sandford Lido celebrated its fiftieth anniversary. The open-air pool was built on allotments that abutted the 14-acre Sandford Park and swimmers first took the plunge there on 25 May 1935.
(Brian Donnan Photography)

Demolition of the castellated Salvation Army Citadel in Bath Road began in 1988. For some months members of the Army congregation worshipped in St Luke's Church hall, while the mothers and toddlers met at St Matthew's. The youth group found a temporary home at Pilley Baptist Chapel and the band rehearsed at the Army hall in Swindon Road. All these activities came back under one roof when the new Citadel was completed in February 1989. *(Brian Donnan Photography)*

In December 1983, the Playhouse Theatre was the venue for *Rome Sweet Rome*, a panto produced by the Friends drama group. Leading lights in the group were members of Decameron, a folk-rock band of Cheltenham-based musicians that enjoyed success in the 1970s and 1980s. *(Brian Donnan Photography)*

Opposite: In February 1984, the former site of Parry's wood yard in Ashford Road was developed. Terraced houses and a block of flats occupy the land today. This view looks across the site from the corner of Grafton Road to the Jolly Brewmaster pub in Painswick Road. *(Brian Donnan Photography)*

White Christmas in the promenade, 1981. *(Brian Donnan Photography)*

The 1990s

The dramatic fly-past by RAF Tornados of a funeral at St Philip &
St James's Church, Leckhampton, was captured on film in July 1993. The
church opened in 1882 and its saddleback tower was added a few years
later. Its architect, John Middleton, was responsible for other Cheltenham
churches including St Mark's, All Saints and St Luke's. *(Brian Donnan
Photography)*

An aerial view of Cheltenham in the mid-1990s. The High Street cuts a swathe through buildings to the left. The Whitbread tower fronted by the open space of the former Black & White coach station is just to the right of centre. And the Prince of Wales stadium occupies the top right-hand corner. *(Brian Donnan Photography)*

113

Considered an eyesore almost from the day it was built in 1954, Royal Well bus station eventually bit the dust in October 1998. Scrub and trees were removed shortly afterwards, allowing the elegance of the crescent to be appreciated by onlookers for the first time in half a century. *(Brian Donnan Photography)*

Royal Well bus station after the makeover. *(Author's collection)*

Cheltenham Grammar School, photographed just before its demolition in 1996, was designed by London architects Chamberlain, Powell and Bon. Work started in November 1962 and the school opened at Easter 1965. Despite its rugged appearance, the building survived barely three decades. By then the dreaded concrete-cancer, to which many a 1960s structure fell victim, had taken terminal hold. The 'squatting toad', as it was once described in a letter to the *Echo*, was reduced to rubble, to be replaced by a more modest building in the contemporary superstore style. *(Author's collection)*

Looking down Regent Street from the High Street prior to pedestrianisation. The corner building will be remembered by some as a town centre pub called the Regent Bar, then the Continental Bar. *(Brian Donnan Photography)*

Hats and headscarves in the High Street at half past eleven on a slushy winter day in the early 1990s. *(Brian Donnan Photography)*

Beechwood Place construction site, looking towards Albion Street in 1990. The land had previously been home to Woolworths and Haines & Strange garage. *(Joe Stevens)*

Beechwood Place opened its doors to shoppers in March 1991. The development cost £35 million, but four years later its owners, the Church Commission for England, sold the mall to the Universities Superannuation Scheme Ltd for just £15 million. *(Joe Stevens)*

Madame Wright's in the Little Promenade shut up shop for the last time in the '90s. Until the end, this gown shop with its glorious art deco façade continued to close on Wednesday and Saturday afternoons as it had for many years. Nothing so common as a price tag was ever seen in the window of Madame Wright's. If you needed to know how much it cost, you couldn't afford it. *(Joe Stevens)*

In this aerial view from August 1995, the Park Campus of Gloscat (Gloucestershire College of Art and Technology) can be seen in the lower right-side quarter. At the end of the '90s plans were announced to sell off this site for housing and relocate the college at Hesters Way on land formerly occupied by Monkscroft school. *(Brian Donnan Photography)*

Gloscat, Park Campus. *(Author's collection)*

Members of the Cheltenham and County Cycling Club ranged across the Prom in 1990. The Christmas trees outside the Municipal Offices tell us at what time of year the pedallers posed. Left to right: Matthew Barnes, Lawrie Hunt, Rob Zelenka, Dave Birt, Maurice Stray, Matthew Harris, Alan Moss, John Stammers, Tim Sluman, Terry Morgan, Martin McGreary, Tim Davies, Nick Peatson, -?-, Mike Tarling, Julian Frankland, Brian Donnan. *(Brian Donnan Photography)*

The Spa Shuttle arrived in – and departed from – Cheltenham in the late '90s. Three 'Noddy trains', as the shuttles soon came to be called, were bought at a total cost of £429,000 to provide a free ferry service to travellers around the town centre/Montpellier/Pittville areas. The annual running costs were £250,000. Some saw the gas-powered road trains as a far-sighted attempt to address the problem of traffic congestion. Others felt the Noddy trains made the problem worse by reducing the speed of vehicles in their wake to a snail's pace. But the greatest objection was cost and the Noddy trains were withdrawn in September 1999. *(Brian Donnan Photography)*

Crowds of schoolchildren gathered to welcome the Queen when she arrived at Lansdown railway station, October 1993. The uniformed figure standing behind the royal visitor is Henry Elwes, Lord Lieutenant of Gloucestershire. GCHQ was the Queen's first port of call, followed by a tour of Wall's ice-cream factory in Gloucester. *(Brian Donnan Photography)*

In August 1997, an exhibition of work by the Cirencester-based artist Sophie Ryder was staged around the town. This impressive rabbit took up residence in Imperial Gardens, along with a flock of metal sheep. After the exhibition the bunny hopped it and the sheep moved to pastures new, but Sophie Ryder's Hare and Minotaur stayed. Thanks to a group of enthusiasts who raised the necessary £50,000, the enigmatic statue can now be seen on the Prom's pedestrianised stretch. *(Brian Donnan Photography)*

GCHQ, Benhall. Plans to bring together GCHQ's Benhall and Oakley locations were discussed during the decade. Two options were shortlisted for the new government communications centre – either to build at a new site in Barnwood, or redevelop the Benhall site. The latter was chosen and work on the 'Doughnut', as the new building was dubbed when plans were shown, began in 1999. *(Brian Donnan Photography)*

The town bade farewell to a family-run retailer of long standing when Holyoake & Son of Bath Road closed towards the end of the decade. Facing towards Oriel Road, the grocery store took pride in a well-presented window and lovely wrought ironwork around the first floor windows. *(Joe Stevens)*

121

At the end of the '90s the former Daffodil cinema in Suffolk Parade was imaginatively converted into a restaurant. *(Author's collection)*

A good example of late '90s architecture, the flats built on the St Paul's college site celebrate the junction (a Victorian idea) of Clarence Street and St George's Place. *(Author's collection)*

Developing the Broadwalk in the 1990s gave Imperial Square the completed appearance that it had lacked before. Built on land adjacent to the Queen's Hotel, the Broadwalk is in sympathy with its neighbours – even down to the detail of heart and honeysuckle ironwork around the balconies. *(Brian Donnan Photography)*

St James's station site, February 1999. Compare this with the 1970 view on page 93 and you'll see that apart from the office block, which was built for Mercantile & General, not much had changed. However in 2000 – just thirty-five years after the site became vacant – large-scale development was under way. *(Brian Donnan Photography)*

Some appalling architectural mistakes made in the 1950s and '60s scar Cheltenham to this day. So have lessons been learned? Here's the Millennium restaurant in Portland Street, Gold Cup day, March 1999. *(Brian Donnan Photography)*

And here's Century Court in Bath Road. The people who live in these flats have the daily pleasure of looking at the elegant buildings of Cheltenham College directly opposite. *(Author's collection)*

Acknowledgements

Many thanks to the following people who loaned pictures and helped with information for this book:

Joan Ashton
Josie Chilton
Dave Avery and Andrea Print, Gloucestershire Constabulary
Brian Donnan Photography
Anita Syvret and Sue Robbins, *Gloucestershire Echo*
Jean Hewitt
Isabel Syed, Eagle Star
Peter Stephens
Joe Stevens

War Weapons Week, when this sound detector was placed on view in the Prom, November 1940. Like all pictures of sensitive subjects, this *Echo* photograph had to be sent to the censor before publication. This one never appeared. 'Not to be published' read the words, initialled in red on the back of the picture, endorsed by the censor's stamp. (*Gloucestershire Echo*)

Sandford Lido
1935 - 1985